Kousalam

Interview Mantras

SUDHANSHU PANI

JASASWINI MISHRA

CONTENTS

INTRODUCTION

In India if you have reached the stage of Interview it is 70% battle won. Given the large number of candidates who apply for each position, you should be happy that you have been called for an interview. But the challenge now is more certain and it is going to be intense competition. Be rest assured that for each position there would be atleast 10 deserving candidates. However, there are a few steps that could give you a slight advantage. The purpose of this book is to help you avoid known pitfalls that could end in a bad interview and equip you with certain skills to help you perform better.

RESEARCH THE COMPANY

Companies like candidates who know what they want. They are also impressed with someone who has done some digging before arriving at the interview. Make the effort to research your target organization, and you'll find yourself ahead of the competition. It is a part of Commercial Awareness. Your employer would be impressed if they find you keen to learn more about the company, products, its business environment, competitors etc. Given two equal candidates, the one who shows the most interest usually wins.

Today most organisations have an informative website and you could also find some additional material on search through search engines. If the company is listed the amount of information you find is usually higher. The company would have quarterly and annual regulatory filings and reports. They would also have communication to current and prospective investors.

ACTION:

Go through them and make notes

Rehearse a pitch or a monologue using the newly gained information

.

KNOW YOURSELF

In an interview you are trying to sell yourself. You can do that only when you have thoroughly understood your own self. Your abilities, constraints, desires, aspirations, motivation, dreams, personality, interests, future goals etc.

Once you are more aware, you can apply these insights to explain to the target company regarding your suitability. If you do not think you can contribute to their success skip the interview. If you think you can, figure out how and why. Connecting the two successfully is the best way to get yourself hired. Above all else, be authentic.

An employer can intuit your sincerity and true level of interest and commitment. There are no right or wrong answers, your awareness about yourself would bring out the stronger aspects of your personality and skill sets.

You're "selling" your skills and yourself as a person. First: Your skills. An easy way to uncover yours is to list your accomplishments and then think of which skills it took to do them. Did baby-sitting require psychological sensitivity? Did selling kitchen knives require skills of persuasion? Review your list, and refine your skills into a "package" you can explain easily in a minute or two.

Next: You as a person. Most organizations want honest, smart, friendly, motivated, and responsible employees. Do you deal well with people? Are you flexible and open to learning? Did you, for example, show determination to get back on the slopes after you broke your leg skiing? Again, after you make your list, refine it so you can explain your personal "assets" in a minute or two.

ACTION:

Brainstorm and practice speaking about these for 1-2 minutes.

Practice regularly. Do mock interviews or attend some interviews just to get some practice.

PRACTICE. PRACTICE. PRACTICE

If you are an experienced bloke you may need less practice. However, if you are a fresher you need more and more. There's no substitute for rehearsing how you'd handle an interview.

Ask your parent, sibling, colleague or best friend to be the interviewer, and give her or him a list of questions to throw at you. There are ways to handle each of these. If you know what they are before you're in the "hot seat," your confidence going into the interview will soar. And remember, if you get a question that you can't answer, simply say you don't know. If you can attempt to speak or guess it, speak it and inform that it was only a guess.

Do inform the interviewer that you would look into the question and that you are willing to learn what it takes. Again, an employer will respect someone who is honest and open about his or her limitations.

Body language is the other thing to be well aware of. If you have a video camera, use it for the practice; otherwise a mirror will do. Hand and arm movements shouldn't be too large. Don't fiddle. Your posture should be relaxed, but alert. Don't slouch; if you look bored in the interview why wouldn't the recruiter presume that you'd then be bored in the job too? Communicate interest and energy. Be yourself. If your demeanour can reflect positivity, energy and enthusiasm it would take care of any mistakes / errors you may make while 'answering' questions.

Clichés aside, practice does make perfect; it works for interviewing too.

DRESS APPROPRIATELY

You have to wear the attire that is expected in the industry or company you are appearing for the interview. In case you do not know, go in formals or simply ask them for a suggestion. With any organization, the way to dress is the way you would dress if you got the job.

Personal grooming is part of your "dress" too. A good haircut or trim will impress. So will clean fingernails, a fresh-scrubbed look, pleasant breath, and a smile. And please, no perfume or aftershave ... you might love how you smell with that scent, but others may not!

GET THERE ON TIME

This may seem obvious, but if you're not on time for your interview, the game is over. Getting there early allows you to take a few deep breaths, organize your notes, refresh your memory on a few points that you've found difficult in your practices, and scan any company materials that may be available in the waiting room. It also allows you to answer the "call of nature" (if there is a call) and to make any last-minute appearance adjustments. Usually, you may lose your composure in case you are late due to traffic or any other exigencies. Hence plan and reach a little early so that you take care of uncertainties.

The result? You'll feel better about yourself, and you'll be more relaxed in the interview. So leave plenty of time, and get there early. It gives you a psychological edge and demonstrates your professionalism.

MAKE AN IMPRESSION

First impression is very important. It may seem cruel, but first impressions can be deal makers... or breakers. The interviewer starts forming opinions from the moment the two of you shake hands. The handshake is indeed critical. Practice it.

Look the interviewer in the eye as you offer your hand. Shake his or her hand firmly ... but not like a vise. Smile at the same time, and say something enthusiastic like, "Hello Mr. Raman, it's great to meet you!" or "Hello Ma'am, I am delighted to meet you!"

As you walk to his or her office, make some small talk-- team or sports scores, how great the lobby looks, a recent storm... you get the gist. Initial Ice-breakers would settle your nerves. Establish positive vibes and the rest of the interview will feel more natural and less like you're being grilled at Viva / College practicals.

ANSWER WELL

You're going to be asked some questions. It is important that you answer them well. Your answers should make sense and be logical and coherent.answering them well:

Don't ramble. It's better to give a shorter answer with strong points in it than to babble on for five minutes in a disorganized fashion.

Look the interviewer in the eye when you're answering. If you don't, he or she may think you're fabricating your answer right there on the spot.

Gather your thoughts. If you need a minute to collect your thoughts in order to answer a specific question, feel free to say: "I need to think about that for a moment ... " or "That's a great question ..." The interviewer will respect your honesty and your desire to offer a thoughtful answer. If a question is a difficult one, try to remember how to approach it. If you blank out, be honest, but definitely put a positive spin on your answer. A little humor never hurts either. You may always ask the interviewer for clarifications in case you have not clearly understood the question.

ASK QUESTIONS

Usually at the end of an interview, you'll be asked if you have any questions. If you don't ask something, it can be taken as a sign of lack of interest . . . so prepare some questions before the interview. Since you will not get all information about the organisation or your job in your research, there usually would be a number of questions in your mind. There are two areas to question -- the organization and the job itself. We recommend asking about the job first. Are you clear on the responsibilities of the job? If not, ask for clarification. The clarity of thought and doubts that you portray would convey more about you than perhaps your answer. Of course, your interest in the job or organisation should always reflect in your tone and expressions.

Do you see where the job fits into the structure of the organization? Do you understand whom you'll be working with, and what their expectations of your work are? By the way, do not ask about the salary or benefits -- vacation, holidays, sick days, etc. -- in the first interview. Leave that for after they have presented you with an offer.

Be sure you know what the next steps are after the interview. Are they going to contact you? When do they think they can do that? Would they prefer you to follow up with them? How is the best way to do that?

The end of the interview is also a good time to emphasize how interested you are in taking the process to the next step and why you think you'd be the perfect candidate for the job. Do not beg for the job, but let your positive energy and enthusiasm win the day. Upon leaving, make sure to shake the person's hand again and make sincere eye contact. And, of course, don't forget to thank him or her.

BE YOURSELF

This is the most important step. No matter what anyone says, you can't pretend to be someone you're not. Believe me, even the best actor may not be able to pretend. We always think we can pretend and the interviewer cannot see through. But in important roles this is never the case. Trained interviewers spot actors quickly.

In the interview, let who you really are shine through. Be proud of that precious collection of talents, motivations, and skills that make you the individual that you are. Believe in your ability to learn, grow, and develop, and act accordingly. Show "the real you" -- sense of humor and all -- and you'll be well on the way to getting hired.

BE HONEST

Don't fudge your answers. Don't fudge your resume. Short cuts will not take you too far.

GIVE EXAMPLES

Examples, illustration, data and stories are the best way to make a point. It's one thing to say you can do something; it's another to give examples of things you have done.

Prepare a dossier of examples of the work you have done. Arrive at your answers on what you have done from the examples. The interviewer would typically ask you questions in areas related to the role. Try to anticipate and mull over instances in your work experience that can form the examples. If it is recent and important for the organization then better. Answer with specifics to the questions asked. Give instances and examples that display or demonstrate your skill, experience or exposure to the Interviewers question.

BE CONCISE

Interviewees sometimes lose track of the point in the interviewer's question. Also it may be the natural way of conversation of some individuals to beat around the bush without coming to the point. Rambling on is one of the most common interview blunders. Listen to the question and answer it concisely and precisely. If you have a weakness in this area and you too go off on a tangent after hearing the question, learn to answer to the point.

KEEP YOUR GUARD UP

Recruiters are mostly experienced in their Art. Some of them would approach the interview in a formal and Q&A style format. They would expect you to maintain the same level of seriousness and professionalism in the Interview Process.

Other recruiters may have a more conversation style approach and may try to make the candidate more comfortable. Some recruiters may also get very friendly and non-formal in their approach. A trick used by some of them to induce you to lower your guard. As a thumb rule you need to ensure a basic and measured level of professional and formal approach to your stance so that you do not go wrong or get caught in the wrong foot.

FOLLOW UP

Your interview isn't over when you walk out the door. As soon as you get home, write a short thank-you note to your interviewer. If somebody in the organization had set up the interview for you, call him and thank him for the same and update him of the events. If any person was co-ordinating you can speak to them or write to them and the interviewer. You appreciated the time they spent with you and the chance to learn more about the job and the organization, so tell them.

If you promised to send something additional --writing samples or another copy of your resume, for example -- make sure to enclose it. Keep your note short, and restate your understanding of the next step. If you'd like to add something you forgot to say, this is the time and place. Ask if you should be following up later.

You'd be surprised how many candidates never offer this simple bit of courtesy. Send a thank-you note, and you'll stand out in the crowd.

COMMON QUESTIONS – SIMPLE ANSWERS

We end this book on Interview Mantras with some common and hence important questions. We try to analyse some simple answers for these questions.

Why don't you tell me about yourself?
Tell us more about yourself

These are standard and classic interview questions. Once you are an interviewer, you too may start your session with this question. What is the idea here. The question thrown to you is an unstructured and generic question. How you handle yourself would demonstrate your ability to handle such situations. There are no right or wrong answers, it is about how you handle yourself. The confidence you exude, how articulate you are and what is the first impression you are able to create.

Another objective of this question is to put you at ease by

offering you your most familiar territory. So if you are aware about yourself or you have practiced enough it is the easiest answer for you.

Of course the recruiter wants to know more about your career graph, your career choices, what you look up to in a job and your motivations in life and profession.

Usually candidates find this question a difficult one to answer. This is because you do not know what the recruiter is expecting to hear. And you probably know too much about yourself. But here is your opportunity and you should grab it with two hands. You have the chance to take the initiative and describe yourself positively and focus the interview on your strengths. You have the opportunity to quash any pre-conceived notions the recruiter may have about you. Be prepared to deal with it.

The best way is to focus on your strengths and accomplishments and also to include what you think would interest the interviewer. You need not ask the recruiter about why he or she is asking this question. The recruiter may prompt if she wanted to know about something specific. Whatever you say deliver with confidence. It will impress the interviewer.

The interviewer is primarily interested in your professional details.

While she may discuss your personal details, it is of lesser importance. Start with your most recent employment and explain why you are well qualified for the position in discussion. Such a basic thing this is. The key to all successful interviewing is to match your qualifications to what the interviewer is looking for. You want to be selling what the buyer is buying. How well equipped you are professionally to handle the role and represent the organisation in the position is what is to be highlighted. Be specific, concise and give examples if possible.

Understand your Important Accomplishments and Highlight in the Interview

Story telling is an art. Each one of us need to atleast master our story. And the story should necessarily illustrate your best professional qualities. For example, if you tell an interviewer that people describe you as honest or sincere or a turnaround specialist you need to go on and explain how these have helped you achieve your goals and how these have benefitted your erstwhile or present organisation.

A good story can leave a lasting impression and overlook certain handicaps and shortcomings you may have. Get better with your story every day.

How long have you been with your current (or former) employer?

This is an extremely important topic for people in their mid-careers. Employers sometimes have tolerance for short job stints or job hopping at early stage of your career but not so if any pattern or trend emerges. Most employers would not shortlist you in such circumstance. You will have to work extremely hard to wrest the initiative in case you get the opportunity despite this handicap. Nothing in this book can help you if your résumé reflects considerable job-hopping.

Employers expect employees to take up challenges in the job and personal life and try to deliver on the goals. None of this can happen in 1-2 years. Excellent performers tend to stay in their jobs at least three to five years. The best employees are survivors expecially when things are not in their favour. They implement course corrections, bring in new resources, and, in general, learn how to survive—that's why they are valued by prospective employers.

Do clarify your resume to the interviewer in case changes in your resume were not induced by you. Companies closing down, bought over, moving out or simply changing the name.

The bottomline is you need to rectify the tenure issue with your current or prospective employment. People who know you may be inclined to favour you with opportunities.

What is your greatest weakness? What are your strengths?

The interviewer would always assume you have presented your best story. Sometimes if the interviewer feels that you are unable to clearly explain your strengths he may ask you about it. He would mostly ask you about your weakness. If you can give a confident and good response it shows your preparation, self awareness and ability to evaluate your weakness and try to improve or take steps to not let it impact the organisation goals and performance. Remember you cannot hide your weakness after you join an organisation, be sincere in your answer. If your weakness is of great significance so as to affect your performance in the role you need to overcome it or better not go in for such a role. Tell the recruiter what you are doing to overcome it. Keep things concise, simple, straight and short. Dont blabber. Keep this planned and execute.

Tell me about a situation where you did not get along with a superior.

Give any instance or opinion you have in this subject. The recruiter wants to check how you deal with people and situations when there is a difference of opinion or when there is stress and friction in the team. Everyone encounters these situations. If you haven't your experience is not well rounded and there is a chance that you may not be in a position to deal with adverse situations like when you are in disagreement with your boss.

How have you dealt with failure and set backs
Describe an experience when you have failed

When you are in the early part of your career this question is not of great significance to prospective employer. But for leadership roles it is very important. Again no right or wrong answers. You do score points if you have the experience of such situations. The world of business is not perfect, the idea here is to check how well you have been polished by experience. If you can't discuss a failure or mistake, the recruiter might conclude that you don't possess the depth of experience necessary to do the job.

The recruiter would try to evaluate your ability to assume responsibility, to be a team player, to lead in crisis, your decision making skills and your ability to recover from a mistake or setback and your ability to inspire others in the organisation.

Explain what such episodes have taught you and what you have learnt. Give examples and stories to aid your points.

Do specify and elaborate if such episodes benefitted the company in any way. Be brief.

How do you explain your job success? Career growth etc

Dont sound arrogant. You may mention the observation of your mentors or supervisors or peers about your strengths.

What do you do when you are not working? What are your hobbies etc

It is very important to have hobbies and activities to develop a wholesome personality. The more senior the position, the more important it is for the recruiter to know about the candidate's qualities that will impact his or her leadership style. Is the person a workaholic or balanced, well adjusted and happy, social, physically sound etc.

Discuss hobbies or pursuits that interest you, such as sports, clubs, cultural activities, and favorite things to read. Specifically mention activities that take up bulk of your personal time and things that you are passionate about. These should be a point of information only don't get into discussion or argument regarding anything related to your likes or interests.

Why did you leave your last position?

For senior level roles it is important if you are getting along with all stake holders. Issues relating to your personality and temperament become important for leadership positions. Will you fit in with the company's culture. Do you have a personality problem.

Again be positive, honest and straightforward. Nothing is right or wrong, if the recruiter does not think you would be a right fit because of personality issues, perhaps he is doing a favour to your career. Highlight positive developments that resulted from your departure, whether it was that you accepted a more challenging position or learned an important lesson that helped you to be happier in your next job.

Recruiters particularly would be perplexed if you have in the past left organisations that they themselves hold in high regard. Be sensitive to such observations and be precise in your answers.

Why do you want to work in this industry?

Create a story around this. What attracts you. How it relates to your strengths. Why did you become interested. Point out any similarities between the job you're interviewing for and your current job. You need to impress the interviewer that this is a carefully thoughtout and considered career move and not simply a job shopping. Does this move gel with your career plans and aspirations. Is your story consistant with your entire story.

ABOUT THE AUTHOR

Sudhanshu Pani is currently a banker and associated with the Kousalam Project as a mentor. He has over 15 years of experience as a professional in leading organizations in India and as an entrepreneur with Finance Central.

Jasaswini Mishra is Co-founder of **'Kousalam – The People Skill Project'** . She was earlier associated with SIES College of Commerce, Mumbai as a Professor.

This book is a part of the Series **Career Planning – The Kousalam Way**. It is intended to aid the users of the Kousalam Career Planning App.